Pharaohs, Pyramids, and Mummies

by Anna Keyes

Table of Contents

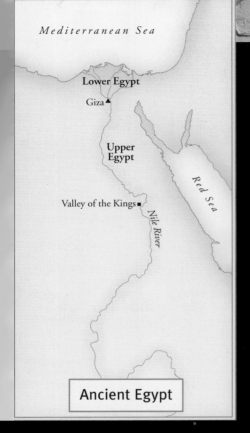

Ancient Egypt

Introduction

About 5,000 years ago, one of the earliest **civilizations** in history arose. It was a farming society, based around the Nile River, and faced by deserts on three sides. The Nile flooded every year and enriched the soil. Farmers grew wheat, flax, and other crops in this rich soil. They also raised animals for meat. Children helped care for the livestock while their parents worked in the fields.

Today, this civilization is known as ancient Egypt. It lasted from about 3000 B.C. to 1000 B.C.

IT'S A FACT

The Nile River is the longest river in the world at 4,160 miles (6,695 kilometers). It was the center of life in ancient Egypt. Historians have called it "The Great Highway" because people used it to transport almost everything.

Starting around 3000 B.C., ancient Egypt was ruled by a series of kings. Each king was called a **pharaoh** (FAY-roh). A pharaoh was a supreme ruler who owned all the land in the kingdom. A pharaoh was also the chief religious leader. Ancient Egyptians believed that a pharaoh was a god in human form. They believed that when a pharaoh died, he became part of the god Osiris (oh-SIGH-ruhs).

Most pharaohs were men. Only a few were women. Female pharaohs were considered to be kings, not queens. One pharaoh, King Tutankhamen (toot-ahng-KAH-muhn), was only nine years old when he became king. Another, named Ramses (RAM-seez) II, ruled for 67 years.

This painting shows the god Osiris (on left) with a pharaoh (on right).

A newly discovered stone coffin gets dusted off.

The ancient Egyptians believed in life after death. They believed the bodies of the dead would be needed in the afterlife. Ancient Egyptians preserved bodies as **mummies** and placed them in burial structures, or **tombs** (TOOMZ). They put food and possessions in the tombs with the mummies.

Because of their status as gods, the pharaohs' preparation for the afterlife was done on a grand scale. Their tombs were bigger and more expensive than those of common people. Some of the pharaohs' tombs were in the form of great **pyramids**.

Many of the pyramids and tombs of ancient Egypt have been explored by **archaeologists** (ahr-kee-AHL-uh-jihsts). These are scientists who study ancient people and their culture. Archaeologists also study mummies. Even after thousands of years, mummies can reveal how people died and give clues about how they lived.

In this book, you will meet some of the most famous pharaohs. You'll learn about the great monuments they had built. You will learn about the treasures and the mummies found inside Egypt's pyramids and tombs. As you read, notice how important death and the afterlife were to ancient Egyptians.

Now let's begin our journey to the past and explore ancient Egypt—the land of pharaohs, pyramids, and mummies.

This special gold coffin held the internal organs of a pharaoh.

Pharaohs Rule!

The pharaohs were totally responsible for what happened in their kingdom. As the religious leader, the pharaoh was the connection between the Egyptians and their gods. As the military leader, the pharaoh's duty was to protect Egypt from its enemies and expand its power. In addition, the pharaoh was a lawmaker and judge. Pharaohs had complete power over Egypt and its people.

Yet the life of a pharaoh was a life of luxury. Pharaohs lived in huge palaces filled with elegant furniture and art. Some palace grounds contained pools, gardens, and even a zoo. When pharaohs went to temple ceremonies, servants carried them on chairs made of gold and jewels.

stone carving showing a pharaoh driving a chariot

Who was the first pharaoh? The answer is a bit of a mystery! Many ancient writings refer to the first king as Menes (MEE-neez). But there are few traces of a real person named Menes. Some historians think he was actually King Narmer.

Whatever his real name was, he is remembered as the leader who united Upper and Lower Egypt. Before 3000 B.C., 600 miles of land along the Nile was divided into two parts: Upper Egypt and Lower Egypt. (See map on page 2.) Menes was the king of Upper Egypt. When he conquered Lower Egypt, he united the two lands. As its pharaoh, he ruled one of the first nations in history.

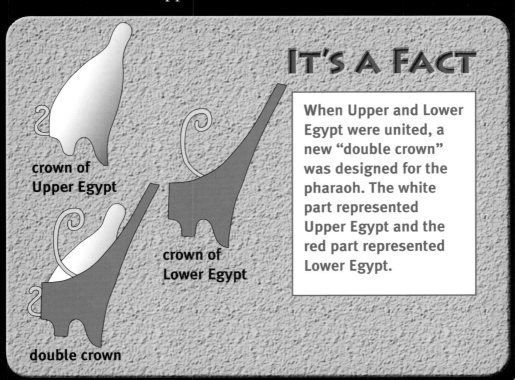

crown of Upper Egypt

crown of Lower Egypt

double crown

IT'S A FACT

When Upper and Lower Egypt were united, a new "double crown" was designed for the pharaoh. The white part represented Upper Egypt and the red part represented Lower Egypt.

This is the Great Pyramid of Giza in Egypt.

One of the most famous pharaohs of ancient Egypt was King Khufu (KOO-foo). He is known for the tomb he had built for himself, the Great Pyramid at Giza (GEE-zuh). This pyramid is the largest pyramid ever built. It is about half as tall as the Empire State Building in New York City. Some of its blocks weigh as much as nine tons.

Some stories say Khufu was a bully, or worse, who treated his people poorly. Perhaps these stories are just legend, inspired by the sight of the awesome pyramid. People might think that only a bully could force workers to build such a huge monument in his honor.

The most famous female pharaoh was Hatshepsut (hat-SHEP-soot). She ruled Egypt along with her stepson. During her life as a pharaoh, Hatshepsut sent armies to conquer nearby lands and people to trade with other nations. After she died, her stepson, Thutmose (thoot-MOH-suh) III, became pharaoh. He wanted people to forget that she had been a king. He wanted to be remembered as more powerful and important than Hatshepsut. So he had many of her monuments and images destroyed.

IT'S A FACT

Hatshepsut understood that it was very uncommon for a woman to be a pharaoh. She had artists paint pictures showing her with a man's body and a woman's head. She often appeared before her people wearing a false beard.

portrait head of Hatshepsut

The pharaoh Akhenaten (ahk-NAH-ten) made a change in Egypt's religion. For many years, Egyptians had been worshiping several different gods. Akhenaten wanted this to stop. He chose the sun god, Aten (AHT-n), and made Aten the only god of Egypt. Many Egyptians, including many of the priests, did not approve of the new religion. They did not want to worship only one god.

THEY MADE A DIFFERENCE

Amenhotep III (ah-mehn-HOH-tehp) is remembered as one of the most successful pharaohs of ancient Egypt. He is known for his numerous building projects as well as his diplomacy, or skill in handling foreign affairs. During his reign, Egypt enjoyed a time of economic well-being. Amenhotep knew that Egypt's great wealth was tempting to the rulers of nearby lands. He could have used warfare to keep other rulers from invading Egypt. Instead, he used diplomacy. The pharaoh sent written messages to communicate with other rulers. The written messages were small carvings on clay tablets, which became known as the Amarna (uh-MAHR-nuh) letters.

Akhenaten is remembered for more than his worship of the sun god. He is also remembered because of his wife, Queen Nefertiti (nehf-uhr-TEE-tee). She is thought to have been one of the most beautiful women in history. Akhenaten put many paintings and statues of her in his temples and monuments.

In 1912, a German archaeologist discovered a statue of Nefertiti. He was so amazed by her beauty that he wrote in his journal: "Description is useless—see for yourself."

limestone bust of Queen Nefertiti

IT'S A FACT

The ancient Egyptians used a kind of picture writing called **hieroglyphics** (hye-ruh-GLIH-fiks). It's a complex system. Some hieroglyphs have more than one meaning. For example, the hieroglyph for "one million" is a picture of a man holding up his hands in the air. The picture also means "I can count no further!"

11

✓ POINT

▲▲▲▲▲▲
▲▲▲▲▲▲

Talk It Over
Why do you think Tutankhamen relied on the suggestions of his advisors? If you were a pharaoh at a young age, would you use advisors to help you make decisions? Why or why not?

Howard Carter emerges from the tomb of Tutankhamen holding a box of artifacts discovered there.

Perhaps the most famous pharaoh is King Tutankhamen. He was only nine years old when he became pharaoh. The boy-king faced a big problem in his new role. His people were still unhappy about worshiping only one god, as Akhenaten had ordered them to do. Tutankhamen's advisors pressured him to change this rule. Tutankhamen agreed to let the Egyptians return to their worship of many gods.

Until 1922, the world knew little about the life of Tutankhamen. Then a British Egyptologist named Howard Carter discovered Tutankhamen's tomb.

When Carter first opened Tutankhamen's tomb and looked inside, he could barely speak from amazement. Although grave robbers had stolen from the tomb, they left behind many of its treasures. More than 5,000 objects, many of them covered in gold, filled the four-room tomb. These artifacts had been untouched for centuries. Carter found clothing, jewelry, trumpets, and swords and daggers. He found chariots and models of ships. The tomb even contained the boy-king's toys and games. A jewel-covered throne from the tomb is one of the most valuable objects ever found.

The discovery of the tomb of Tutankhamen was one of the most exciting events in the history of archaeology. It was big news throughout the world.

decorated throne of Tutankhamen

Primary Source

Howard Carter, the Egyptologist who discovered Tutankhamen's tomb, kept a diary of his amazing discoveries. On November 26, 1922, he wrote that when he was asked if he could see anything as he entered the dark tomb, he said, "Yes, it is wonderful."

Ramses II, or Ramses the Great, had the longest reign in Egyptian history. At a time when most people lived only for about 30 years, he lived for about 90 years. His reign lasted almost 67 years. He had many wives and might have fathered more than 100 children.

This great pharaoh is remembered for his building programs and the power of his armies. His many military successes increased Egypt's wealth. Ramses II was so admired that many pharaohs who came after him changed their names to Ramses!

A statue of the pharaoh Ramses II stands among the ruins of Luxor Temple in Egypt.

Pyramids and Tombs

The pyramids of ancient Egypt are some of the most famous structures of all time. They were built as tombs for the pharaohs. As a burial place, the pyramid would protect the body of the dead pharaoh so its *ka*, or "life force," could pass on to the afterlife.

Deep within the pyramid, a secret burial chamber for the pharaoh lay at the end of a narrow passageway. Workers carved religious spells on the walls of the tomb to help the pharaoh's passage to the afterlife. Other rooms within the pyramid contained food, furniture, jewelry, and other supplies that the pharaoh would need in the afterlife. Paintings adorned the walls.

Valley of the Kings

IT'S A FACT

Grave robbers stole many of the rich treasures from the pyramids. This might have been why many pharaohs were buried in tombs in a remote valley instead of in pyramids. This valley is known today as the Valley of the Kings.

Why did the ancient Egyptians use the pyramid shape for their tombs? We may never know for sure. One story is that the pyramid was like a mountain to the sky. It would allow the pharaohs to climb to the heavens after they died.

The first pyramid was built for the pharaoh Zoser. It is called the Step Pyramid because it looks like a series of giant steps.

THEY MADE A DIFFERENCE

Imhotep (ihm-HOH-tehp), who designed the Step Pyramid, was the first architect to build in stone instead of mud bricks. Imhotep was thought to be one of the wisest men in ancient Egypt. He knew much about medicine as well as architecture.

The Step Pyramid of Zoser was finished about 2648 B.C.

The Bent Pyramid was built between 2625 B.C. and 2585 B.C.

It was not easy to build a true pyramid. Unlike a step pyramid, a true pyramid has a square base and four smooth sides that come to a point at the top. The first attempt was not successful because the sides were too steep and the pyramid began to collapse. The architect had to change the slant of the sides. This first true pyramid is called the Bent Pyramid because of its odd shape.

The Pyramid Builders

It took so many workers to build a pyramid that whole towns were put up to house them. Archaeologists found the remains of a workers' town that could house up to 20,000 people. The workers were fed with fish, beef, and bread. Many of these workers were farmers. Every year, the Nile flooded the surrounding land from July to September. Since the farmers couldn't work on the flooded land, free food and housing in exchange for pyramid work might have been a good deal.

Exactly how workers built the pyramids is still a mystery. Some archaeologists think workers may have used large sleds to slide gigantic blocks of stone over wet ground. Perhaps pulleys and ramps were used to position the heavy stones. Workers may have built a dirt ramp next to the pyramid to provide a way to move the heavy stones into position.

The largest of Egypt's pyramids is called the Great Pyramid, which was made for King Khufu. This tomb included more than just the pyramid and its burial chambers. Boats that were meant to carry the pharaoh into the next life surrounded the Great Pyramid.

The Great Pyramid stands 449 feet (137 meters) tall. This tomb consists of about 2 million blocks of stone. The average weight of one of its blocks is 2.5 tons, although some weigh as much as 9 tons. Although it used to have an outer facing of smooth limestone, most of that is gone now.

the three pyramids of Giza

Menkaure's pyramid

Khafre's pyramid

Great Pyramid (Khufu's pyramid)

The Great Sphinx

A **sphinx** is a mythical creature that has the body of a lion and the head of a man. The Great Sphinx guards the pyramid of Khafre at Giza. One of the legends about the Great Sphinx involves Thutmose IV. When he was a prince, Thutmose had a dream about the Sphinx. In the dream, the Sphinx told Thutmose to remove the sand that had piled up over the Sphinx. If he did this, the Sphinx said that Thutmose would become king. When Thutmose followed those instructions, he did become king.

Khufu's Great Pyramid is one of the three pyramids at Giza. This complex of pyramids was a family affair. Khufu's son, Khafre (KHA-frah), had his pyramid built next to his father's pyramid.

Nearby Khafre's pyramid sits the huge figure of the Great Sphinx. The pharaoh Menkaure (mehn-KOO-ray), son of Khafre, built the third pyramid at Giza.

Making Mummies

The ancient Egyptians believed that a person's spirit and body would be reunited in the afterlife. It was very important, therefore, to preserve the body so the soul could recognize it and rejoin it. This is why the Egyptians turned their dead into mummies.

The first mummies were probably created by accident. Early Egyptians buried their dead in the sand. The sand dried out the bodies and preserved them. But animals sometimes disturbed the dried bodies. To protect the bodies from animals, Egyptians began to bury their dead in coffins.

This mummy is believed to be the pharaoh Ramses I, the father of Ramses II.

Without the sand to dry them, the bodies decayed in the coffins. This worried the ancient Egyptians. How would a soul recognize its body after death? The Egyptians had to come up with a way to preserve the bodies. So about 2600 B.C., they developed a process called **mummification**.

The process took about 70 days. First, the body would be washed with wine and some water from the Nile. The Egyptians believed that this washing would purify the body. Next, the body was **embalmed**, or preserved, by a

priest. This involved removing many of the internal organs from the body. The organs from the stomach area were removed first, because they decayed very quickly.

IT'S A FACT

Egyptians considered cats to be sacred. There are many examples of cats being mummified in ancient Egypt. Some were even buried in cat-shaped coffins!

This mummy of a pharaoh is displayed in the Egyptian Museum in Cairo, Egypt.

Egyptian statue of a cat

The liver, stomach, intestines, and lungs were carefully washed and placed in **canopic** (kuh-NOH-pihk) **jars**, which were buried with the body.

Ancient Egyptians thought the heart was the center of intelligence. They left it in the body to be used in the afterlife.

They believed that the gods would weigh the dead person's heart. If it weighed more than a feather, the gods knew the person had done many bad things. The person would not be allowed to have an afterlife. The heart would then be eaten by a god-beast that had a crocodile head and hippopotamus legs.

IT'S A FACT

Ancient Egyptians thought the brain was unimportant. During the embalming process, the brain was taken out of the head with a hook inserted through the nose. Then the brain was thrown away.

The lid of this canopic jar represents a god with the head of a falcon.

After the organs were removed, the body was packed in a salt substance to dry it out. Forty days later, the embalmers washed the body again. Then they rubbed it with fragrant oils to keep the skin from drying out too much. After that, they wrapped the body in long linen strips. **Amulets**, or charms, were hidden inside the linen to protect the body from evil.

Finally, the linen was coated with resin. This sticky substance kept the wrappings glued down and helped preserve the body.

IT'S A FACT

To make mummies look less sunken after the organs were removed, embalmers would stuff the bodies with dry rags. They even added false eyes to the mummies to make them look more lifelike.

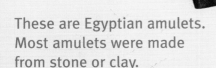

These are Egyptian amulets. Most amulets were made from stone or clay.

23

What happened after mummification? It depended on how wealthy the dead person had been. People such as the pyramid workers would be buried in simple wooden coffins. A wealthy person would be placed in a wooden coffin that was nested within other wooden coffins. These were then placed in a **sarcophagus** (sahr-KAHF-uh-guhs), or decorated stone coffin. The sarcophagus would then be placed in a tomb.

Also in the tomb were objects that would help the dead person in the afterlife. People who were not wealthy were buried with only a few items, such as beads and jars of food. Wealthy people had fancier burial chambers, filled with their valuables. Of course, pharaohs had the fanciest burial chambers and the most valuables of all.

This mummy is in the Toledo Museum of Art.

The ancient Egyptians treated their dead very well. They prepared the bodies for the afterlife. They provided the dead with protective amulets and spells. Egyptians placed food and other objects in the tombs of the dead. They even wrote letters to their dead relatives and placed them in the tombs. The ancient Egyptians did all this to keep their dead happy and to help them into the afterlife.

IT'S A FACT

In ancient Egypt, the richer you were, the fancier your funeral could be. Dancers and special ceremonies were some of the extras that money could buy. Families that were wealthy even paid people to weep at the funeral!

Sculptures such as these were placed in tombs as guardians.

Ancient Egyptians believed in curses. As a warning to grave robbers, people would place curses inside tombs. It was rumored that one of the bricks in Tutankhamen's tomb had a curse written upon it. This curse, according to the rumor, promised death to anyone who opened the tomb. A few people died shortly after the opening of the tomb, including the man who paid for the dig. Some people actually believed that the curse had power! But when experts studied the writing on the brick, it turned out that it was not a curse after all.

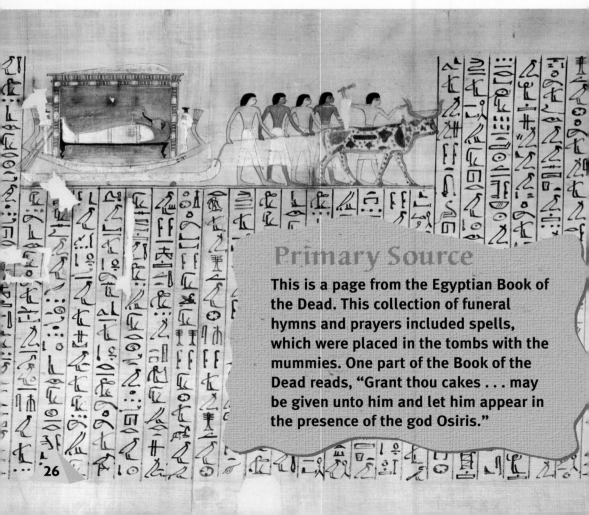

Primary Source

This is a page from the Egyptian Book of the Dead. This collection of funeral hymns and prayers included spells, which were placed in the tombs with the mummies. One part of the Book of the Dead reads, "Grant thou cakes . . . may be given unto him and let him appear in the presence of the god Osiris."

IT'S A FACT

In 1974, the mummy of Ramses II was flown to Paris for a medical exam. The Egyptian government issued the mummy a passport. On the passport, Ramses' job was listed as "King (deceased)."

An Egyptologist removes salt deposits from a mummy.

Scientists can learn a lot by studying an ancient Egyptian mummy. They can estimate how old the person was when he or she died. They can see evidence of some types of injuries. For example, scientists often see broken bones in the mummies of the pyramid builders. That's not surprising, considering the hard physical labor performed by these workers. Scientists can also see evidence of diseases the person had, such as plague and smallpox.

When scientists examined the mummy of pharaoh Ramses II, they learned that he was about six feet tall. This was unusual for the time; the average ancient Egyptian was about five feet tall. They also learned that Ramses suffered from battle wounds, arthritis, and weak circulation.

Conclusion

Archaeologists and other scientists have learned much about ancient Egypt by studying its pyramids and tombs as well as the artifacts and mummies within them. They've learned about ancient Egyptians' lives and their belief in the afterlife. By studying mummies, scientists have learned much about how those people lived.

A worker brushes dust from a 2,000-year-old mummy.

✓ POINT

Read About It
You can read more about pharaohs and pyramids at your school media center or local library. An adult can help you find more information on the Internet.

Archaeologists learn about life in ancient Egypt by studying paintings such as this one. It shows the inspection of cattle.

In this book, we've learned that preparation for the afterlife was important to ancient Egyptians. We've learned that pharaohs had pyramids built in preparation for the afterlife. And we've learned that building the pyramids provided work, food, and housing for many people.

Are there still mysteries to solve in ancient Egypt?

Certainly! For example, there is still much to learn about how the pyramids were built. As scientists continue to study mummies using modern technology, perhaps they will learn more about diseases of that time period. Ancient Egypt keeps us searching for answers and treasures of all kinds.

Pharaohs of Ancient Egypt

3000 B.C.	Menes unifies Upper and Lower Egypt.
2686–2648 B.C.	Zoser has Step Pyramid built.
2625–2585 B.C.	Sneferu reigns, builds several pyramids, including the Bent Pyramid.
2585–2560 B.C.	Khufu reigns, builds the Great Pyramid at Giza.
2555–2532 B.C.	Khafre reigns, builds second pyramid at Giza.
2532–2510 B.C.	Menkaure reigns, builds third pyramid at Giza.
1479–1458 B.C.	Hatshepsut reigns alongside Thutmose III.
1479–1425 B.C.	Thutmose III reigns.
1390–1353 B.C.	Amenhotep III reigns.
1353–1336 B.C.	Ahkenaten reigns, changes Egypt's state religion.
1332–1322 B.C.	Tutankhamen reigns, returns Egypt to state religion.
1279–1213 B.C.	Ramses II reigns.

(All dates are approximate.)

Glossary

amulet	(AM-yuh-liht) a charm worn as a protection against evil (page 23)
archaeologist	(ahr-kee-AHL-uh-jihst) a scientist who studies ancient people and their culture (page 4)
canopic jar	(kuh-NOH-pihk JAHR) a jar that held the preserved organs of a mummy (page 22)
civilization	(sihv-uh-lih-ZAY-shuhn) the way of life of a particular people, nation, region, or period (page 2)
embalm	(ehm-BAHM) to treat a dead body with preservatives to prevent decay (page 21)
hieroglyphics	(hye-ruh-GLIH-fiks) Egyptian picture writing (page 11)
mummification	(muhm-uh-fih-KAY-shuhn) the process of preserving and wrapping a body for burial (page 21)
mummy	(MUHM-ee) a body that has been preserved and prepared for burial (page 4)
pharaoh	(FAIR-oh) the title of an ancient Egyptian king (page 3)
pyramid	(PIHR-uh-mihd) a shape that has a square base and four triangular sides that meet in a point (page 4)
sarcophagus	(sahr-KAHF-uh-guhs) a coffin made of stone (page 24)
sphinx	(SFIHNGKS) a mythical creature having the body of a lion and the head of a man (page 19)
tomb	(TOOM) a room beneath the ground used for burial (page 4)

Index